sbya

DRUGS & CONSEQUENCES

THE TRUTH ABOUT
STEROIDS

LARRY GERBER

ROSEN
PUBLISHING

New York

Published in 2014 by The Rosen Publishing Group, Inc.
29 East 21st Street, New York, NY 10010

First Edition

Library of Congress Cataloging-in-Publication Data

Gerber, Larry, 1946–
The truth about steroids/Larry Gerber. — First edition.
    pages cm. — (Drugs & consequences)
Includes bibliographical references and index.
ISBN 978-1-4777-1895-7
1. Steroids—Physiological effect—Juvenile literature. 2. Steroid drugs—Juvenile literature. 3. Steroid abuse—Juvenile literature. 4. Doping in sports—Juvenile literature. I. Title.
QP752.S7G47 2014
572'.579—dc23
                                        2013018666

Manufactured in the United States of America

CPSIA Compliance Information: Batch #W14YA: For further information, contact Rosen Publishing, New York, New York, at 1-800-237-9932.

CONTENTS

It's hard to imagine many people who would choose to be weak if they could be strong. If there's a choice, who would want to look like a geek when they could be muscled up? What if the choice was getting cut from the team versus being a star?

The answers are all the same, of course. Just about anybody would pick the star body and the star role. What if it was possible to get that body in just a few months? If all you had to do was take a few pills or shots?

Anabolic steroids seem like a good deal to a lot of people, whether they play sports or just want to look good. Steroids are the only widely abused drugs that are not intended to get you high, but to change your body.

Anabolic steroids and weight training make muscles grow faster. Steroids can be taken as pills, injections, skin creams, and patches. However, even the biggest steroid fans admit that they are not wonder drugs. It still takes work to build muscle, with or without steroids. And steroids don't make anybody faster or smarter.

Anabolic steroids are serious trouble for any-one who hasn't finished growing. Some people argue about whether steroids are as dangerous for adults as they're reported to be, but anyone

There's no secret formula. The body produces its own natural steroids, which help build muscle. The right diet and workout routine are key.

who knows anything about steroids knows they are trouble for teens. That would be true even if they were legal.

It's against the law to have or sell steroids without a prescription in the United States and many other countries. The U.S. government puts them in the same class as heroin and methamphetamines. Even so, they're easy to find in many places, and they can be ordered on the Internet by anyone who's willing to take a chance on getting busted or ripped off.

Using steroids can be a tempting idea. Stars in practically all kinds of sports have won medals, championships, and millions of dollars after getting help from steroids. Some got caught and some didn't. Some succeeded beyond their wildest dreams, but for others the dream turned out to be a nightmare. Some have paid with their lives.

The tale of how steroids entered the American sports world reads in places like a spy thriller. Other parts of the story are all about science, especially the chemistry of the human body. Some parts are right out of a sci-fi horror movie, where mad doctors and the secret police treat kids like human guinea pigs.

It's not just about sports; it's also about star quality. Many steroid users simply want to look good or be strong. One of the most famous steroid users, Arnold Schwarzenegger, was a bodybuilder, movie star, and governor of California.

There are so many steroid stories that it can get confusing, especially because there are so many gym experts and Internet gurus who claim to know more about steroids than most doctors do. In some ways they may be right because doctors and scientists can't carry out experiments on humans, while steroid users experiment on themselves.

It's sometimes hard to know what to believe. Maybe the best place to start is to take a look at the drugs themselves. Exactly what are steroids, anyway?

1

What Are Steroids?

People need steroids—not to win championships or medals in sports—but to grow and function in a natural way. Steroids are chemicals produced naturally in the human body.

Steroids are just one type of the chemicals known as hormones, which are found in all animals and plants. Hormones act as messengers. They tell cells when to do certain things, triggering natural changes in their organisms. In mammals, hormones are carried in the bloodstream from one part of the body to another.

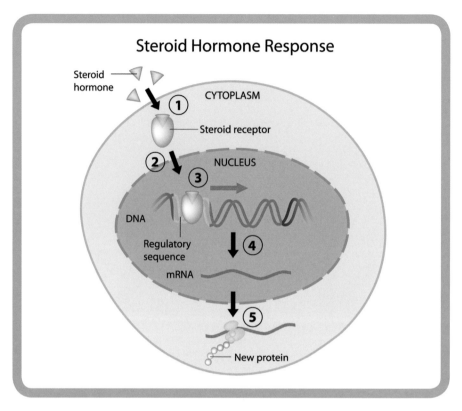

Steroid Hormone Response

Steroid hormones help build muscle by interacting with DNA in the nucleus of each cell. This interaction creates protein, which promotes growth.

Testosterone

The principal male hormone is the steroid testosterone. In men, testosterone is produced mostly in the testes, although the adrenal glands of both men and women also produce small amounts. Men's bodies naturally create much more testosterone than women's.

Testosterone stimulates the development of male sex organs, and it's responsible for male physical characteristics such as beards, body hair, and deep voices. It also stimulates the growth of muscle and bone tissue.

People have known for a long time that castrating an animal, or removing its testes, would stop development of its male characteristics and make the animal less aggressive. Experimenters in the 1800s and early 1900s used tissue or extracts from human and animal testes in attempts to treat a variety of medical problems.

However, it wasn't until 1935 that scientists isolated the hormone testosterone. Soon afterward, they figured out how to make synthetic testosterone in laboratories. Researchers in Germany and Switzerland won the 1939 Nobel Prize for chemistry for their work with hormones, particularly testosterone.

Researchers found that the body changes testosterone into many different chemical compounds, and they called this group of compounds androgens, meaning things that produce male characteristics. They also discovered that some steroids are anabolic—meaning that they build muscle tissue.

During and after World War II in 1940s, steroids were used to treat battle wounds and burns, and to help patients recover from surgery. Starved victims of concentration camps were given steroids to help rebuild their bodies. Doctors also saw some of the problems steroids could cause, especially in women. Female patients developed facial hair and deeper voices.

Chemists were able to create new steroid compounds that reduced these androgenic effects, but they were never able to eliminate them completely. That's why the full name for this class of drugs is anabolic-androgenic steroids, often abbreviated as AAS.

Not All Steroids Are Anabolic

Bad publicity about sports cheating and abuse of anabolic steroids has led to confusion about the whole steroid family. Some people are even wary of taking steroids that are prescribed by their doctors, even though these steroids are not anabolic or androgenic.

Actually, most of the steroids used in medicine are another branch of the steroid family, called corticosteroids. These are often used to treat inflammation from injuries, arthritis, asthma, and other problems in both men and women.

The female hormones estrogen and progesterone are other examples of steroids that are not anabolic or androgenic. Synthetic versions of these hormones are prescribed to women for birth control and treatment of premenstrual syndrome.

To make things more confusing, several kinds of widely used performance-enhancing drugs (PEDs) are not exactly anabolic steroids, although they may be chemically related. These types of PEDs include androstenedione ("andro" for short), human growth hormone (HGH), and erythropoietin (EPO).

Steroids and other performance-enhancing drugs are a big industry, even though they're illegal without a doctor's

A LONGTIME USER SPEAKS OUT AGAINST STEROIDS

When he got to college, Lyle Alzado didn't think he would make it in football because he wasn't big enough. So in 1969, he started taking anabolic steroids. He went from 190 pounds to 220 pounds (86 kilograms to 100 kg) by eating a lot, but he said the steroids helped him bulk up to 300 pounds (136 kg).

He went on to play defensive end in the National Football League (NFL) for fifteen years. He made All-Pro twice and earned a reputation as one of the meanest, toughest players in football.

Alzado died in 1992 of brain cancer. He was forty-three years old. Before he died, he told anyone who would listen that his health problems were caused by a steady diet of steroids. He told about having fits of rage on and off the field and said steroids made him act "crazy."

All-Pro NFL defensive end Lyle Alzado died of cancer after a career of heavy steroid use.

He testified in Congress, urging U.S. lawmakers to pass stricter laws against steroids, which they eventually did.

Alzado used steroids almost nonstop during his playing days. At the end of his career, he also took human growth hormone to try a comeback. It didn't work.

"Whoever is doing this stuff, if you stay on it too long or maybe if you get on it at all, you're going to get something bad from it. I don't mean you'll definitely get brain cancer, but you'll get something. It is a wrong thing to do," Alzado wrote in a *Sports Illustrated* article.

"I know there's no written, documented proof that steroids and human growth hormone caused this cancer," he wrote. "But it's one of the reasons you have to look at. You have to. And I think that there are a lot of athletes in danger."

prescription in the United States, Canada, and many other countries. There are many more steroids available on the black market than there are for medical uses, and the doses taken by athletes and bodybuilders are often many times greater than a doctor would prescribe for a medical condition.

Steroids Come to America

The first synthetic steroids were developed in Europe, and doctors soon found they could be used to help patients recover from injury and illness. The story of how they came to be widely used in America sounds like something out of a spy thriller.

In 1954, Vienna, Austria, was host to the World Weightlifting Championships. At the competition, athletes from the Soviet Union amazed everyone with their huge lifts and their over-sized muscles.

During this time, Vienna was still recovering from World War II and was notorious as a city of spies and black marketers. It was occupied by foreign armies, including Americans and Russians who opposed each other in the Cold War. In this atmosphere of suspicion and intrigue, U.S. weightlifting team doctor John Ziegler met quietly one evening with the Soviet team doctor in a Vienna bar.

Ziegler knew the Soviet lifters were onto something new, but he didn't know what. Over drinks, he asked the Russian doctor about his training methods. The Russian admitted to Ziegler that his lifters were being given testosterone.

When he returned home, Ziegler began experimenting with testosterone on himself and on his friends at a weight club in York, Pennsylvania. They didn't like the effects of testosterone. Ziegler began working with a new compound, which was later sold under the trade name Dianabol. It was one of the first synthetic anabolic steroids.

Doctors prescribed Dianabol for burn victims and elderly patients, but its main users were competitive weight lifters and bodybuilders. Ziegler spread the word about his discovery to other athletes, and Dianabol use spread as well. At the time, there were no rules against using steroids in competition.

Dianabol was one of the first synthetic anabolic steroids in sports. Many other compounds are available today, but Dianabol is still widely used.

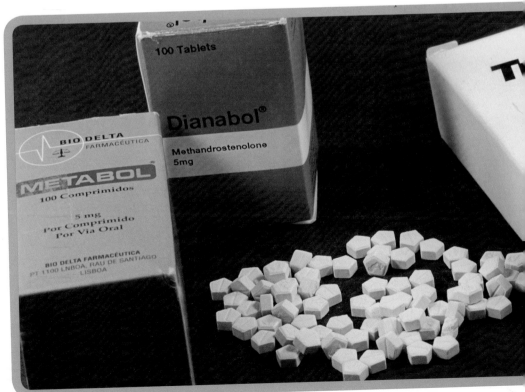

Ziegler came to regret his work as a steroid pioneer. He blamed his own later ill health on steroid use, and he got disgusted when he learned that athletes were taking far higher doses than he recommended.

Young Athletes Become Human Guinea Pigs

As steroid use spread in international athletics, Olympic spectators scratched their heads over the success of athletes from the German Democratic Republic, or East Germany. The small nation of sixteen million regularly won more medals than countries ten times bigger. Furthermore, some East German athletes looked superhuman. Opponents sometimes challenged female East German athletes to prove that they really were women because many of them looked so masculine.

After the country's communist government fell in 1989, records of its secret police were opened. They revealed one of history's biggest doping operations, which had been carried out on the nation's young athletes.

Top officials who wanted to show the superiority of their system in international sports gave steroids and other performance-enhancing drugs (PEDs) to more than ten thousand athletes. They included girls as well as boys, some of them as young as eleven.

Hundreds of East German doctors and chemists did research on new forms of PEDs and on ways to beat drug

Andreas Krieger was Heidi Krieger, the woman in the picture, when he won the European shot put championship. He says the steroids he was forced to take destroyed his female identity.

tests for international competitions. Many of the victims were told the steroids were vitamins. Some were threatened for asking too many questions.

The results were a nightmare for many athletes, whether they won medals or not. Some developed cancer and liver failure. Women later had miscarriages and deformed babies. Heidi Krieger, the 1986 women's European shot put champion, said the steroids destroyed her female identity. She had a sex change operation and became a man, Andreas Krieger.

Two leaders of the doping program were later tried and convicted of causing harm to a sample group of 142 women, but they weren't given severe punishments. A fund was also set up to give some compensation to the athletes. Many of them, saddled with high medical bills, said it wasn't enough.

CHAPTER 2

Phony Champions

Performance-enhancing drugs are nothing new in sports. Greek athletes training for the ancient Olympic Games drank and ate all kinds of potions and plants. They ate animal testicles for strength, though of course they didn't know about testosterone.

In modern times, steroids came into sport through the weight room. No matter what sort of steroids a person takes, he or she won't build muscle unless they work out properly. Training will build muscle without steroids, but steroids won't build muscle without training. The muscle-building properties of steroids were obvious early on to weightlifters and bodybuilders.

Since the first Olympic doping tests for steroids in 1976, at least thirty-six weightlifters have been disqualified, more than in any other sport. Bigger, stronger muscles aren't the only reason that steroids can give athletes unfair advantages, however.

Some steroid compounds can increase the kidneys' ability to produce erythropoietin, or EPO, which increases the red cell count in human blood. A higher red cell count allows oxygen to be transferred more efficiently through the body so that an athlete can train harder and longer than he or she normally could.

Bodybuilders pose at the Arnold Classic in Brazil. The event was named for Arnold Schwarzenegger, a pioneer bodybuilder who used steroids before they became illegal.

That has made steroids—as well as synthetic EPO itself —
popular among elite cyclists who want to cheat, and there have
been many of them.

PEDs in Cycling and Track

Lance Armstrong, who won the Tour de France a record seven
times, was stripped of his championships for using testosterone,
EPO, and HGH. He was only the latest in a long string of bike
riders caught doping. The 1998 Tour de France, the world's pre-
mier bike race, is still known as the "Tour de Farce." Customs
officials found testosterone, EPO, and other drugs in a team car
and team warehouse.

Riders staged a sit-down strike to protest the crackdown,
and many quit or were disqualified. Only 96 of 189 starters
finished the race. Fans were disgusted, and the sport of cycling
has never been quite the same.

Track and field sports have also had major steroid problems.
Canadian sprinter Ben Johnson amazed the world in 1988
when he ran the Olympic 100 meters in a world record 9.79
seconds. After officials found the steroid stanolozol in his urine,
he was disqualified and his record was erased. His coach later
claimed that practically all of Johnson's competitors were doping, and several of them were indeed implicated in later drug
scandals.

American sprinter and long jumper Marion Jones had to
return her five Olympic gold medals after admitting in 2007

Olympic track and field gold medalist Marion Jones cries outside court after admitting she used steroids. She was sentenced to six months in prison for lying to investigators.

that she used steroids and other PEDs. She was sentenced to six months in prison for lying to federal investigators about her steroid use.

Jones later apologized in public for using steroids and lying about it. She founded a program called Take a Break, which encourages young people to stop and think about the possible consequences before doing something they might regret.

Jones was just one of many star athletes involved in a huge steroid scandal known as the BALCO case. Some of its best-known figures were baseball players.

Baseball and the BALCO Scandal

Baseball fans and sportswriters began to suspect some top major league players of using steroids or other PEDs in the late 1980s. Commissioner Faye Vincent put steroids on baseball's list of banned substances, but he wasn't able to get team owners and players to agree on a program for testing.

Suspicion continued to grow over the next ten years as more and more players kept hitting more and more homers. In 1996, seventeen players hit at least forty home runs, by far the highest number in history. Some sportswriters accused owners and the players union of ignoring players' steroid use.

Two years later, St. Louis Cardinals slugger Mark McGwire admitted using androstenedione after a jar of the "pre-steroid" substance was found in his locker. Andro wasn't on the banned list at the time, and McGwire went on to hit seventy homers. His record didn't last long.

The Bay Area Laboratory Co-Operative, or BALCO, was a company based in Burlingame, California, which made nutritional supplements. Federal authorities suspected the company of supplying illegal PEDs to athletes and began an investigation in 2002.

The biggest star implicated in the BALCO case was San Francisco Giants slugger Barry Bonds. In 2001, Bonds set

Victor Conte, founder of BALCO, was sentenced to prison for selling steroids and money laundering. He holds a picture of his most famous client, Barry Bonds.

the major league single-season home-run record, seventy-three. His many other records include 762 career home runs.

Bonds was never convicted of using illegal drugs, but he was convicted of obstructing justice. He wasn't sentenced to prison, and he appealed his conviction.

Investigators found BALCO client lists naming athletes in several other sports, including track and field, cycling, boxing, and football.

Football

The 1963 San Diego Chargers are known as football's steroid pioneers. Players were given steroids in training camp. Dianabol pills were served in bowls on team dining tables. These Chargers were also the first NFL team to do strength training in a regular way. They went from a losing season in 1962 to American Football League champions in 1963, behind devastating offensive

JUICED!

Jose Canseco created a sensation with his 2005 book about steroids in baseball.

José Canseco, one of the top major league hitters during the 1980s and 1990s, created a sensation with his best-selling book *Juiced: Wild Times, Rampant 'Roids, Smash Hits, and How Baseball Got Big*. In the 2005 "tell-all" book, he admitted using steroids himself and claimed that many other major league players were using them, too.

Canseco said he gave steroid injections to several other players, including Mark McGwire. Most of the players named in *Juiced* denied his claims at first. However, many of them were later caught "juicing," or admitted they had done so.

Canseco said he became infertile after quitting steroids because his body quit producing his own testosterone. In an ESPN interview, he called himself a "modern-day Frankenstein."

He said he couldn't get a job coaching or doing anything else in organized baseball, and was having a hard time making a living in other businesses because people regarded him as a snitch.

"I definitely regret getting involved with steroids in any way, shape or form," he said.

and defensive linemen who had done preseason weight training on steroids.

Some people still scoff and call that team the "San Dianabol Chargers," but there was nothing phony about their championship. Steroids were perfectly legal at the time. That team was also part of another trend that soon spread throughout sports: weight training. The Chargers hired pro football's first strength coach.

Until then, many coaches in the speed and agility sports—from tennis to baseball—took a dim view of strength training. They worried about athletes getting "muscle-bound"—losing agility and quickness. Teams like the Chargers who put weights into their training routines soon started proving otherwise.

The NFL began testing for steroids in 1987, and dozens of players have been suspended at various times since then for using. But many people suspect that PED use continues in professional as well as college and high school football. Many former players have admitted steroid use.

Another reason for the suspicion is simply that so many players have gotten so big. Before the "steroid era," 300-pound (136-kg) players were rare in the NFL. Now there are several on every team in the NFL and many in college.

Hall of Fame quarterback Fran Tarkenton is just one of many to complain about steroid use in the NFL. He has written about the dangers of steroids in football, and he says lots of people — fans, players, journalists, and team owners and officials—mostly just want to keep quiet about steroid use because they all want the game to go on.

Not much is heard about PEDs in college sports, but many antidoping experts believe they are being used a lot, especially in college football, even though the National Collegiate Athletic Association (NCAA) and some schools do steroid testing. One reason for the suspicion is the rapid weight gains experienced by many college players.

It's almost impossible for someone to add more than 25 to 30 pounds (11 to 14 kg) of lean muscle a year through diet and exercise alone, but some players have gained up to 80 pounds (36 kg) in a single year. Such a huge increase doesn't prove on its own that a player is using steroids, but it's hard to explain otherwise.

Even less is known about steroid use by U.S. high school students. Surveys over the past few years show that the number of teen users could be as high as half a million, although experts say there are probably more than that.

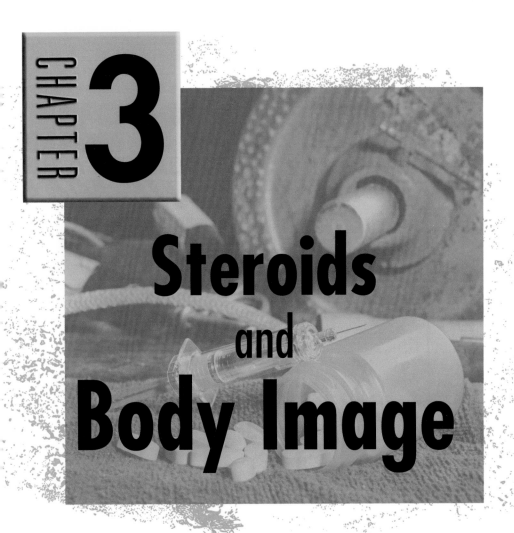

CHAPTER 3

Steroids and Body Image

"Hey Skinny! ...Yer ribs are showing!" Angelo Siciliano figured he could make some money with a pitch like that, and he was right. Siciliano became known to millions as Charles Atlas, and ads for his body-building program appeared in comic books for decades.

The cartoon ads featured a "97-pound [44-kg] weakling." He's on the beach with his girl when a bully kicks sand in his face. His girl laughs at him. The poor guy goes home, kicks a chair in disgust, and starts working out with the Charles Atlas method.

The Charles Atlas ads were successful for many years because of their appeal to guys who felt insecure about looking weak.

Soon he's muscled up and flexing in the mirror. He goes back to the beach, punches out the bully, and gets his girl back. "You ARE a real man after all!" says the last panel.

It's no wonder the Charles Atlas ads were one of the most memorable ad campaigns of all time. They appeal to anybody who might feel insecure about the way they look. Who wants to be laughed at?

It's Not Just Athletes

Steroids are usually associated with sports, but many steroid users aren't athletes. They're people who simply want to be bigger, or look tougher, or more toned. Besides, fitness feels good. And let's admit it, so does being noticed!

However, some people get obsessed with their appearance, and like athletes who cheat, they look for steroid shortcuts to get where they want to be. For some people it's not only a matter of appearance. They may have psychological problems that tempt them to turn to steroids.

Some users have a condition called muscle dysmorphia, a distorted image of their own bodies. Males may think they're small and weak when they're really not. Females may falsely see themselves as flabby when they're actually fairly thin.

The National Institute on Drug Abuse (NIDA) cites other common reasons for steroid abuse. Some who use steroids have been physically or sexually abused. They say they used steroids to get bigger and stronger so that they wouldn't be attacked again. Studies suggest that teens who take steroids tend to take other risks: drinking and driving, carrying a gun, or abusing other drugs.

It's not always about personal image, however. Lots of people use steroids to get ahead on the job. For professional bodybuilders, body image IS the job. Bodybuilders in competition pose before judges and score points for qualities such as muscle symmetry and definition, hoping to win prizes and

High school athletes in Chicago, Illinois, sign a pledge to stay off steroids. They were taking part in a campaign sponsored by former Chicago Bears linebacker Dick Butkus.

sponsorship money. The Mr. Olympia titleholder is generally recognized as the world's top bodybuilder.

Steroids have been a big part of the bodybuilding culture for a long time, but not all bodybuilders use steroids. Several major organizations that are concerned about steroid use hold "natural" bodybuilding competitions. Contestants agree to drug testing or even lie detector tests to prove they haven't trained on steroids.

Anabolic steroids can be tempting for anybody whose job calls for strength. Even police officers have admitted using steroids, and steroids are also abused in the armed forces. The U.S. Army estimated that more than eleven thousand soldiers used illegal steroids in 2007, the latest year for available figures. The army doesn't routinely test for steroids because the tests are expensive.

However, soldiers who get caught using steroids may be reduced in rank or expelled from the service. The army says

ARNOLD PUMPS IRON

What would you think if you heard somebody was doing "Arnolds"? Not long ago, the word just meant a type of exercise—a twisting barbell press for working out the front deltoids. It was named for its inventor, Arnold Schwarzenegger. Today, "Arnolds" is slang for steroids, usually pills.

Schwarzenegger came to the United States from Austria in 1968, when he was twenty-one years old, and became known as the king of bodybuilders. He won the Mr. Universe title four times and was Mr. Olympia seven times.

Steroids were legal at this time, and Schwarzenegger said he got them from his doctor. He told interviewers later that he took them for short cycles to train for big competitions, then stopped using them. He says he didn't use them to build muscles, but for maintenance and muscle definition.

Schwarzenegger was featured in the classic documentary *Pumping Iron*, then went on to be an action superstar in the *Conan* movies and dozens of others, including the *Terminator* films. His movie fame helped him rise in politics to become governor of California from 2003 to 2011.

Schwarzenegger quit using steroids a long time ago, but he continued to work out and stay fit as he got older. His pictures are still featured in muscle magazines and on Web pages. He is credited for turning thousands of people on to weight training and staying fit, but some also blame him for making steroids look attractive to younger people.

A young Arnold Schwarzenegger poses in a scene from the 1969 movie *Hercules in New York*.

any drug use raises questions about whether the soldier can follow orders, and this may also affect the user's security clearance.

Others who may see steroids as a way to get ahead at work include private security workers and nightclub bouncers. Some movie actors do, too, especially action stars whose roles call for muscle.

Sylvester Stallone, an actor, screenwriter, and director, was charged with importing a prohibited substance into Australia in 2007, after authorities said he arrived with vials of human growth hormone.

The Same Old Drug Scene

Some users say steroids give them a sense of confidence and well-being, but most people don't take steroids to get high. Steroids are different from most other illegal drugs in that way. In other ways, however, they're part of the same old drug scene.

There's always the risk of getting caught and going to jail. There's the risk of getting sick—HIV, AIDS, or hepatitis for needle users. There's the risk of getting ripped off by crooked dealers. There's the risk that what you're taking might not be what it's supposed to be, no matter how reliable the dealer.

Then there are the many street nicknames. "Juice" and "roids," are two of the more common ones. "Stackers" and "pumpers" mean types of steroids designed to do certain things or be taken at certain times. "Winny" is short for Winstrol, or stanolozol. "Deca" is Deca-Durabloin, an injectable steroid.

Androstenedione is "andro" for short. Testosterone in product names often gets shortened to "test."

Agents for the U.S. Drug Enforcement Administration (DEA) say laboratories in China manufacture most of the raw powder that goes into steroids used illegally in the United States. The powder is often smuggled to labs in the United States or Mexico, where it's turned into pills or vials for injection. Steroids require a prescription to be sold in Mexico, but many pharmacies there sell them without one. Many of the steroids sold in Southern California, notorious as the U.S. "steroid capital,"

These steroids were seized by authorities in a raid on a house in Florida. One of the people charged in the bust said he sold the drugs to professional athletes.

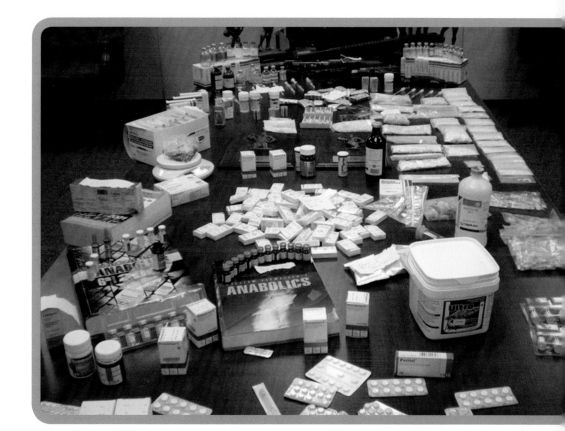

come illegally from Mexico. Steroids worth hundreds of millions of dollars are sold across the United States every year.

It's easy to find steroids for sale on the Internet, but it's not always easy to get what you pay for. Even if the seller actually sends the product as promised, it may be intercepted by law enforcement. U.S. authorities monitor these sites, too, and many illegal importers have been arrested and their shipments taken away.

In addition, there's never a guarantee that what you're buying is what's been advertised. Many black market steroids were intended for use on animals, and many of them are contaminated. Authorities have raided steroid labs where chemicals—intended to be swallowed or injected—were mixed in dirty kitchen sinks.

Resistance training, either with weights or machines, will build muscles without steroids. Experts recommend a proper diet, with a lot of protein, and a day of recovery time between each workout. The body produces its own testosterone, and muscle building is a natural process—it just takes work and commitment.

MYTHS &
FACTS

MYTH "'Roid rage" isn't real.

FACT Medical researchers haven't proved that steroids make people aggressive because they can't test people by giving them bodybuilder-size doses. However, hundreds of people have been arrested for violent crimes after using steroids, even though they had no history of violence before using the drugs. And many users themselves say steroids make them irritable and aggressive.

MYTH Steroids won't stunt your growth.

FACT Teens who take steroids run the risk of being shorter than they would be without steroids for the rest of their lives. High testosterone levels signal the long bones in the legs and arms to stop growing before they normally would, so the user may never reach his full, natural growth.

MYTH There are some steroids that women can take without side effects.

FACT Some steroids are less likely than others to cause face and body hair growth, breast shrinkage, and other male qualities if they're taken in small doses. But everyone's body reacts differently to steroids, and there's always a risk of side effects.

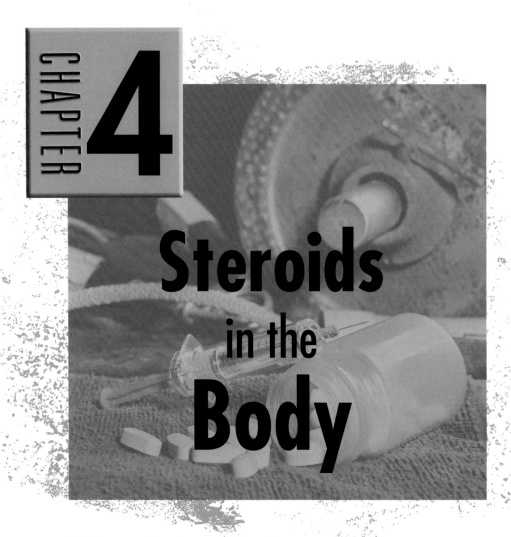

CHAPTER 4

Steroids in the Body

P eople take steroids primarily to build muscles. That doesn't mean that pills or shots will make you stronger, however. Building muscle takes exercise, even with anabolic steroids. So how do they work inside the body?

The Mechanics of Steroids

When an athlete lifts or pulls a weight that's heavier than he or she is used to, the exercise creates tiny tears in the muscle fibers. Even without steroids, the body repairs these tears by adding bigger cells to build a stronger muscle fiber. It's a sort of natural overcompensation. This process is called muscular hypertrophy.

If the process of tearing down and building up is repeated over and over, the muscle will grow. Testosterone is one of the main ingredients in this process, and synthetic steroids add more testosterone into the mix.

These natural or artificial steroids are carried in the bloodstream to a part of each muscle cell called the androgen receptor. These receptors act as doorways, letting the steroid into the cell, where it can interact with the cell's DNA.

DNA is an acid in the nucleus, or core, of each cell. It holds the information organisms need to grow and function. When steroids reach the nucleus, they interact with DNA to stimulate the creation of protein, which promotes cell growth.

By taking different kinds of steroids and varying the amounts taken, athletes can simply add muscle mass—"bulk up"—or they can work toward more fine-toned muscles and go for a more "cut" physique. Using combinations of different types of steroids is often called "stacking."

Increasing and decreasing the amount of steroids taken during training is known as "pyramiding." A user may pyramid by starting a training cycle on small doses, gradually building up the amount of steroids used, then tapering off to nothing at the end of the cycle. A typical "cycling" process goes on for six to twelve weeks.

After the cycle of working out on steroids, it's common for a user to continue training for another cycle without them. Many believe that this allows the body to get back to its normal hormone balance. However, the NIDA says there's no scientific evidence to show that stacking, pyramiding, and cycling actually do what users believe they do.

Medical Uses of Steroids

Because anabolic steroids help build muscles and repair tissue, doctors may prescribe them for patients who have "wasting" diseases such as AIDS, which causes them to lose weight.

Anabolic steroids may also be used to treat anemia, which is a low red blood cell count. Other medical uses include the treatment of breast cancer in women and osteoporosis, or bone loss.

Anabolic steroids may also be given to men who suffer from testicular cancer and need to have the testicle surgically removed. This treatment replaces the testosterone their bodies can no longer make. Steroids can be used to help people recovering from other kinds of cancer and other types of surgery.

Anabolic steroids are also prescribed for male teens who don't start puberty at the natural time. The steroids promote the growth spurt common to early teens and allow them to develop secondary male sexual characteristics, such as a deep voice and body hair.

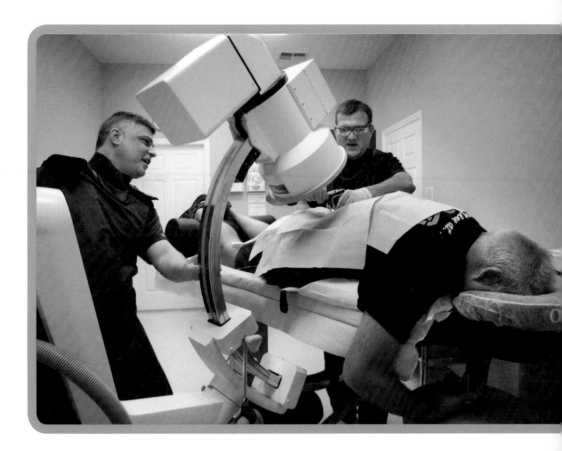

Steroids have several legitimate medical uses. This man is getting an injection during treatment for a back injury.

However, the steroids most used in medicine are corticosteroids, which do not have anabolic or androgenic properties. Corticosteroids work in the body's immune system to reduce inflammation, which can cause pain and restricted movement. They're often given to people with asthma, arthritis, and other conditions, and they may be used to treat injuries as well.

Those Nasty Side Effects

Anabolic steroids do lots of things besides build muscles, and most of them are unpleasant. Some side effects are simply unattractive, such as baldness, pimples, oily skin, shrunken testicles, and breast development in men; and deep voices, face and body hair, and irregular menstrual cycles in women. Some of these problems go away when people stop using steroids, but some, such as baldness and masculine voices in women, are permanent.

Most of the information available on the long-term effects of steroid abuse comes from studies on animals and on case

Steroids sometimes have unwanted side effects, such as rashes, even when they're used under a doctor's care. This patient was taking steroids for asthma.

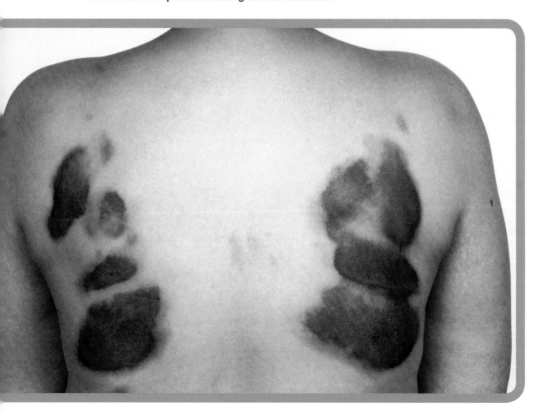

reports about individual humans. So scientists are wary of saying that using steroids will definitely shorten your life. Animal studies suggest that they do, however.

Steroid use is associated with major heart and liver problems. Athletes younger than thirty have suffered heart attacks. Oral steroids in particular affect the levels of low-density lipoprotein—"bad cholesterol"—in the blood and increase the risk of atherosclerosis. This is a condition where fatty deposits are deposited inside arteries, disrupting blood flow.

When blood can't reach the heart, the result is a heart attack. When it can't get to the brain, the result is a stroke. Steroids may also damage the heart muscles themselves.

Steroid abuse is also connected to tumors and blood-filled cysts in the liver. When these growths break, the result is internal bleeding. Infection is a special risk for those who inject steroids. Unsterile needles can cause AIDS and hepatitis. Steroid pills, on the other hand, are hard on the liver and kidneys.

Black market steroids may also be made under unsanitary conditions. Because there are no controls on these steroids' manufacture, most users have no real way of knowing what's in their drugs.

There's been a lot of debate about whether steroids cause mood swings and the outbursts of aggression known as "'roid rage." Many users and former users say they have gotten into fights and committed robbery, vandalism, and other crimes under the influence of steroids. Studies suggest that a minority

TEENS AND STEROIDS: PLAYING WITH DYNAMITE

In 2005, almost seven hundred thousand U.S. high school students admitted using steroids, according to the Census Bureau and the Centers for Disease Control and Prevention. There's debate about whether anabolic steroids can be safe for adults, but there's no argument about their possible effects on teens. Steroids are risky business for anyone who hasn't reached his or her full growth.

There are many potential problems. One is stunted growth. Steroids promote the closure of cartilage called epiphyseal plates at the ends of the long bones in the legs and arms. These plates normally grow throughout childhood and into the teen years, but steroids tend to shut them down. Steroids make testosterone levels artificially high, giving the bones a signal that it's time to stop growing.

However, the most serious steroid problem for teens is death. Don Hooton has studied teen steroid abuse since the suicide of his son Taylor in 2003 and is a recognized expert.

He says depression is a big risk when users quit taking steroids, and it's especially serious for teens because their bodies are already going through big hormonal changes. Taylor had serious mood swings and depression before he decided to kill himself.

Steroids can also lead to serious heart problems, even fatal ones, and they increase the risk of stroke and heart attack even for young users. Those risks come in addition to all the side effects for adult users. They make problems like pimples and baldness look minor.

It's one thing for someone to take steroids if he or she is over twenty-five and knows the risks and still wants to take them, Hooton says, but teenagers who do are "playing with dynamite."

of users may get overly aggressive and irritated. It is believed that some steroids, but not others, affect people this way.

Studies have also shown a possible connection between the abuse of steroids and other drugs. Some addicts have told researchers that they turned to heroin to handle the irritability and sleeplessness brought on by steroids.

Are Steroids Addictive?

Some steroid users also get depressed when they stop taking them, and there have been cases of suicide. Taylor Hooton, a high school pitcher from Plano, Texas, hanged himself in his bedroom in 2003 after periods of steroid use.

His parents said he had severe mood swings and depression when he stopped taking the drugs. They created the Taylor Hooton Foundation to educate young people about the dangers of steroids. Its Web site is http://www.taylorhooton.org.

The site has a long list of warning signs that someone might be using steroids. Some

Don Hooton warns that steroid use is especially dangerous for teenagers. His son Taylor got depressed after he quit taking them and committed suicide at age seventeen.

of the signs are physical, such as unusually fast muscle growth, breast growth on males, bad breath, pimples, hair loss, and greasy skin. Others are mental and emotional, such as extreme mood swings, sudden aggression or irritability, withdrawing from family, lying, or becoming disrespectful or abusive.

There's some debate about whether steroids are addictive. Some users say they were able to use steroids and quit without major withdrawal symptoms. However, the NIDA says they can be addictive. Some users crave more and more as time passes, and they have a hard time quitting even though the drugs are causing physical, mental, and social problems.

Withdrawal symptoms may include depression, mood swings, fatigue, restlessness, loss of appetite, loss of sleep—and a desire to take even more steroids. The most serious symptom is depression because it can lead to suicide, and depression can last for up to a year after the user stops.

Quitting steroids suddenly can be dangerous. Many long-term users kick the steroid habit by going through detoxification, or detox, ridding their body of steroids over a period of time. Many detox and rehabilitation centers have a medical staff to monitor their patients' withdrawal. These centers may also offer psychological help and other drugs, such as antidepressants, to help with withdrawal or medicine to restore the patient's hormonal balance.

TEN

1. My coach says I need to put on some weight if I want to start at my position. What's the best way to do that?

2. What sort of training program is best for me?

3. What sort of things should I be eating so I can bulk up better?

4. If a dietary supplement isn't a drug and isn't illegal, what's the harm in taking it?

5. If you give me a steroid prescription for my asthma, does that mean I'll fail a drug test?

6. Are steroid creams or patches safer than shots or pills?

7. I know guys who look great and play great after using steroids. How can they be so bad for you?

8. I've heard that men grow breasts like a woman if they use steroids. Aren't they supposed to make you more manly?

9. Aren't there any steroids that are safe for teens?

10. If testosterone is a natural hormone, what's wrong with putting it in my body?

5

Controlling Steroid Abuse

The Anabolic Steroids Control Act of 1990 placed steroids in the same category as LSD, narcotic pain-killers, heroin, and other "hard" drugs. It's illegal to possess them without a prescription. A first offense is punishable by up to one year in prison under federal law. Selling steroids is a federal felony punishable by up to five years in prison.

Buying steroids on the Internet is especially risky because U.S. customs and postal authorities often conduct "sting" operations to catch the companies that distribute steroids. Buyers usually aren't the target of these investigations, but buyers may be arrested and pressured to testify against the seller. When a company is raided, authorities also confiscate its records, and it's easy for them to see who has been buying steroids.

There are also state laws against steroids, and the penalties vary from state to state. Young, first-time offenders may not get jail time, but they do face other penalties. They may lose their driver's license, be expelled from school, or be suspended from their sports programs.

Tests and Rules

In the years after John Ziegler pioneered Dianabol use, international sports began waking up to the dangers of steroids. However, twenty years passed before they were banned, partly because there were no tests that could detect them. Tests were finally devised in the 1970s, and steroids were banned from the Olympics. The first tests were carried out at the Montreal Games in 1976.

All major sports now have rules against steroids, and many of them conduct regular testing of athletes. Putting rules into place hasn't always been easy, however. Major League Baseball didn't begin random testing until 2004, and penalties for those caught using were still light.

Mark McGwire and others were called to testify about steroids in a congressional hearing before the opening of the

During a baseball game, New York Mets fans with inflatable syringes taunt San Francisco Giants slugger Barry Bonds about steroid use.

2005 season. Lawmakers scolded baseball officials, saying penalties were still too lenient. After the season ended, a tougher policy was put into place. A player caught using steroids could face a fifty-game suspension for the first offense, one hundred games for the second, and a lifetime ban for the third.

But steroid use continued, and so did fan disgust. Stars such as Roger Clemens, Alex Rodriguez, and many others have been named in steroid scandals. In the 2013 annual voting for baseball's Hall of Fame, voters chose no one because all the eligible superstars were suspected of using steroids.

The NCAA says it conducts about 13,500 tests a year on college athletes for PEDs and other banned substances. Some states test high school athletes for steroids, but the practice isn't widespread. One reason is that tests for steroids are so expensive.

A test for many other street drugs such as marijuana costs only about $8, but a test for steroids costs more than $200. Keeping a sport steroid-free means an athlete may have to be tested several times each year. Many states and schools simply can't afford it.

How Testing Works

Most steroid testing is done on urine samples, which will show higher-than-normal testosterone levels if the subject has been taking steroids. However underground chemists are constantly coming up with new steroid compounds to stay a step ahead of drug tests.

For example, in 2003, the year after the BALCO investigation opened, the U.S. Anti-Doping Agency received and analyzed a syringe that still had traces of a new type of steroid, tetrahydrogestrinone (THG). At first authorities didn't know exactly what THG was. Don Catlin, an antidoping pioneer, studied the drug and developed a test for detecting it.

Lance Armstrong celebrates his seventh Tour de France victory in 2005. He lied for years about using PEDs, but finally admitted it. His titles were taken away.

SECRETS AND LIES

For years, cyclist Lance Armstrong faced accusations that he used PEDs, and for years he claimed to be clean. Armstrong won the Tour de France, the world's biggest bike race, a record seven times.

Armstrong was an inspiration to millions of people—and not just cyclists. He survived testicular cancer partway through his career and came back to win more Tour de France victories. He founded the Livestrong Foundation to promote healthy training and lifestyles.

Armstrong liked to point out that he had never failed a drug test, although he was tested many times. However, several competitors and even Armstrong's own former teammates said he used PEDs. Armstrong was accused of bullying or threatening several people who spoke out about his PED use, but the accusations wouldn't go away.

Finally, in 2013, Armstrong admitted to TV interviewer Oprah Winfrey that he took banned substances, including testosterone, HGH, and EPO, before all of his victories. He also admitted taking transfusions of his own blood to boost his red cell count in competition, a banned practice.

Like many other athletes who have admitted using PEDs, Armstrong said he couldn't have won without them because so many of his competitors were doping, too.

During the investigation, 550 athletes were tested, and twenty of them were found to have taken the designer steroid. When it came time for the *Chicago Tribune* to choose its sportsman of the year that year, the newspaper didn't pick an athlete. It chose Catlin.

Catlin founded the first antidoping lab in the United States at the University of California, Los Angles. He later became president of Anti-Doping Research, Inc. The organization tries to uncover new drugs being used by athletes and develop tests for detecting them. Catlin has overseen testing for the Olympics, the NCAA, the NFL, and other sports leagues.

Antidoping authorities now encourage sports groups to keep athletes' test samples in storage for years. This means that if a new designer steroid is discovered and a test is developed, the old samples can still be tested to see if the athlete was doping.

Many PEDs aren't exactly steroids, although they may be similar. Prohormones are compounds that turn to hormones in the body and have effects similar to anabolic steroids, but these effects are less radical. Prohormones were made illegal in the United States in 2004, and they are also banned in most sports.

Androstenedione is a hormone that's used by the body to create testosterone. Called "andro" for short, it became well known in the 1990s as the supplement used by baseball slugger Mark McGwire. Andro was later banned in major sports and listed as an illegal drug, even though it wasn't believed to be anabolic by itself.

HGH and Other Performance Enhancers

Human growth hormone, or HGH, is illegal without a prescription and banned in sports, but for a long time there was no way to test for it. The first blood test for HGH was introduced at the 2004 Summer Olympics in Athens, Greece. Natural HGH decreases as the human body ages. Its promoters and sellers claim it can restore youth to older people.

HGH is secreted naturally in human pituitary glands. It also has tissue-building qualities, and it increases the anabolic qualities of steroids. Synthetic versions of HGH were created in the 1980s for medical reasons.

Erythropoietin, or EPO, is another natural hormone produced by the kidneys. It stimulates production of red blood cells, which carry oxygen to the muscles and lead to better endurance. EPO is often linked to cheating in professional cycling.

Diuretics can also result in a failed test for PEDs. Diuretics help the body get rid of excess water and salt through the urine, and they're banned in most sports because they can be used to "mask" steroids in the body.

Many diet supplements and shakes sold on the Internet may contain steroids or steroid-like chemicals, even though they're not advertised as steroids. As a result, some athletes who test positive for steroids say they didn't know they were taking them.

That's usually no excuse. Many sports organizations follow a policy called the principle of strict liability. This principle means that if a PED is found in an athlete's sample, the athlete is at fault even if he or she didn't mean to take steroids. The Global Drug Reference Online (http://www.globaldro.org) lets users check on products they might want to take to see if they're banned by the World Anti-Doping Agency.

Some people argue that steroids should be legal for adults and that sports shouldn't try to ban them. They say adults who know the risks of steroids should be allowed to take them.

It's doubtful that the laws will be changed anytime soon, however. Even if they are, the dangers for young people are so obvious that steroids will probably always be prohibited for minors.

GLOSSARY

adrenal glands A pair of glands located near the kidneys that release several types of hormone.

agility The ability to move quickly and lightly.

black market Illegal trading of something that's banned or controlled.

bulking up Gaining muscle mass.

cartilage Firm, flexible connective tissue; in children, it is replaced by bone during growth.

compound A chemical substance made up of two or more elements.

hypertrophy Growth of a muscle or organ through an increase in the size of its cells

implicate To connect someone with a crime or other negative activity.

infertile Unable to produce offspring; in a woman, the inability to get pregnant; in a man, the inability to make a woman pregnant.

intrigue The secret planning of something harmful or illegal.

masculine Having the qualities of a man.

miscarriage A condition in which a pregnancy ends too early and does not result in the birth of a live baby.

organism An individual person, animal, plant, or single-celled life form.

pituitary gland A small gland near the base of the brain that produces several hormones; these hormones affect other glands and influence growth and maturing.

press The motion of lifting a weight to shoulder height, then gradually raising it above the head.

puberty The period of life when a person's sexual organs mature and he or she becomes able to have children.

resistance training Regular exercise with weights, machines, or other devices that causes muscles to contract repeatedly, making them bigger and stronger.

secondary sexual characteristics Physical qualities developed in puberty that are different in men and women but aren't involved in reproduction.

sterile Unable to have children because of defective sexual organs; infertile.

stimulate To encourage increased activity or development.

FOR MORE INFORMATION

Anti-Doping Research
3873 Grand View Boulevard
Los Angeles, CA 90066
(310) 482-6925
Web site: http://www.antidopingresearch.org
This organization researches new performance-
    enhancing drugs and develops tests to show
    when athletes have used them. Its site reports
    many of the latest developments in sports
    doping and has information for parents and
    athletes on dietary supplements, energy
    drinks, and other topics.

Canadian Centre on Substance Abuse (CCSA)
75 Albert Street, Suite 500
Ottawa, ON KIP 5E7
Canada
(613) 235-4048
Web site: http://www.ccsa.ca
The CCSA is Canada's central office for informa-
    tion on steroid abuse as well as other drug
    abuse, treatment, and recovery.

Health Canada
Address Locator 0900C2
Ottawa, ON KIA 0K9

Canada

(866) 225-0709

Web site: http://www.hc-sc.gc.ca

Health Canada is the government agency responsible for helping
Canadians maintain and improve their health. It has information and studies on substance abuse, including steroid abuse.

National Federation of State High School Associations

Box 690

Indianapolis, IN 46206

(317) 972-6900

Web site: http://www.nfhs.org

This federation has information and educational programs on
anabolic steroid abuse for students, parents, and coaches.

National Institute on Drug Abuse (NIDA)

6001 Executive Boulevard, Room 5213 MSC 9561

Bethesda, MD 20892-9561

(301) 443-1124

Web site: http://www.drugabuse.gov

The institute publishes facts about substance abuse and drugs,
including steroids, at http://www.steroidabuse.org.

Substance Abuse and Mental Health Services Administration
(SAMHSA)

Box 2345

Rockville, MD 20847-2345

(877) 726-4727

Web site: http://www.samhsa.gov

SAMHSA works to reduce the impact of substance abuse and
mental illness in America. It keeps information databases
and promotes recovery and treatment programs.

Taylor Hooton Foundation

P.O. Box 2104

Frisco, TX 75034-9998

(972) 403-7300

Web site: http://www.taylorhooton.org

Founded in memory of Taylor Hooton, the foundation tries to
prevent steroid abuse by young people. Its site has news
and information about steroids in and out of sports, drug
information, stories about users and their families, and many
other features.

U.S. Anti-Doping Agency (USADA)

5555 Tech Center Drive, Suite 200

Colorado Springs, CO 80919-2372

(866) 601-2632

Web site: http://www.usada.org

USADA is the anti-doping organization for the U.S. Olympic
movement. It tests athletes for steroids and is a center
for information about steroids and sports. It has drug
information, checklists, guides for athletes, and a line for

reporting steroid abuse. It also has pages of information for elementary students at http://www.usada.org /education/youth.

Web Sites

Due to the changing nature of Internet links, Rosen Publishing has developed an online list of Web sites related to the subject of this book. This site is updated regularly. Please use this link to access the list:

http://www.rosenlinks.com/DAC/Ster

FOR FURTHER READING

Assael, Shaun. *Steroid Nation: Juiced Home Run Totals, Anti-aging Miracles, and a Hercules in Every High School: The Secret History of America's True Drug Addiction.* New York, NY: ESPN Books, 2007.

Canseco, José. *Juiced: Wild Times, Rampant 'Roids, Smash Hits, and How Baseball Got Big.* New York, NY: HarperCollins, 2005.

Canseco, José. *Vindicated: Big Names, Big Liars, and the Battle to Save Baseball.* New York, NY: Simon & Schuster, 2008.

Fainaru-Wada, Mark, and Williams, Lance. *Game of Shadows: Barry Bonds, BALCO, and the Steroids Scandal That Rocked Professional Sports.* New York, NY: Gotham Books, 2006.

Freedman, Jeri. *Steroids: High-Risk Performance Drugs.* New York, NY: Rosen Publishing Group, 2009.

Johnson, David. *Falling Off the Thin Blue Line: A Badge, a Syringe, and a Struggle with a Steroid Addiction.* Lincoln, NE: iUniverse, 2007.

Jones, Marion. *On the Right Track: From Olympic Downfall to Finding Forgiveness and the Strength to Overcome and Succeed.* New York, NY: Howard Books, 2010.

Lau, Doretta. *Steroids*. New York, NY: Rosen Publishing Group, 2008.

LeVert, Suzanne. *Steroids*. Tarrytown, NY: Marshall Cavendish, 2010.

Mackel, Kathy. *Boost*. Reprint ed. New York, NY: Speak, 2010.

May, Suellen, and David J. Triggle. *Steroids and Other Performance-Enhancing Drugs*. New York, NY: Chelsea House Publishers, 2011.

Porterfield, Jason. *Major League Baseball: The Great Steroid Scandals*. New York, NY: Rosen Publishing Group, 2010.

Radomski, Kirk. *Bases Loaded: The Inside Story of the Steroid Era in Baseball by the Central Figure in the Mitchell Report*. New York, NY: Hudson Street Press, 2009.

Robson, David. *Steroids*. San Diego, CA: ReferencePoint Press, 2009.

Roleff, Tamara L. *Steroid Abuse*. San Diego, CA: Lucent Books, 2010.

Rutstein, Jeff. *The Steroid Deceit: A Body Worth Dying For?* Boston, MA: Custom Fitness Publishing, 2005.

Thompson, Teri. *American Icon: The Fall of Roger Clemens and the Rise of Steroids in America's Pastime*. New York, NY: Alfred A. Knopf, 2009.

Walker, Ida. *Steroids: Pumped Up and Dangerous*. Broomall, PA: Mason Crest Publishers, 2012.

BIBLIOGRAPHY

Adams, Jacqueline. *Steroids*. Farmington Hill, MI: Thomson Gale, 2006.

Alzado, Lyle. "'I'm Sick and I'm Scared.'" *Sports Illustrated*, July 8, 1991. Retrieved March 20, 2013 (http://sportsillustrated.cnn.com/vault/article/magazine/MAG1139729/index.htm).

Apuzzo, Matt, Adam Goldman, and Jack Gillum. "Steroids Loom in NCAA Football as Testing, Punishment Remain Inconsistent." Associated Press, December 20, 2012. Retrieved March 3, 2013 (http://www.huffingtonpost.com/2012/12/20/college-football-steroids-ncaa-testing_n_2337326.html).

Artz, Matthew. "Fremont Man Warns About Taking Excess Health Supplements." *Oakland Tribune*, December 2, 2009. Retrieved March 1, 2013 (http://www.mercurynews.com/books/ci_13902487).

Beamish, Rob. *Steroids: A New Look at Performance-enhancing Drugs*. Santa Barbara, CA: ABC-CLIO, 2011.

CBS Evening News. "High School Athletes Turning to Steroids." CBS, February 11, 2009. Retrieved March 30, 2013 (http://www.cbsnews.com/8301-18563_162-3617414.html).

Fainaru-Wada, Mark, and Lance Williams. *Game of Shadows: Barry Bonds, BALCO, and the Steroids Scandal That Rocked Professional Sports.* New York, NY: Gotham Books, 2006.

Farrey, Tom. "Conan the Politician." ESPN.com. Retrieved March 3, 2013 (http://espn.go.com/columns/farrey_tom/1655597.html).

Fish, Mike. "Canseco: Steroids Are Overrated." ESPN.com, June 10, 2010. Retrieved March 20, 2013 (http://sports.espn .go.com/mlb/news/story?id=5244705).

Jendrick, Nathan. *Dunks, Doubles, Doping How Steroids Are Killing American Athletics.* Guilford, CT: Lyons Press, 2006.

National Institute on Drug Abuse. "Anabolic Steroid Abuse." NIDA Research Report Series. Retrieved April 2, 2013 (http://www.drugabuse.gov/publications/research-reports /anabolic-steroid-abuse/how-are-anabolic-steroids-abused).

Peters, Justin. "The Man Behind the Juice." *Slate,* February 18, 2005. Retrieved March 3, 2013 (http://www.slate.com/ articles/sports/sports_nut/2005/02/the_man_behind_the_ juice.html).

Robson, David. *Steroids.* San Diego, CA: ReferencePoint Press, 2009.

Sterngass, Jon. *Steroids.* Tarrytown, NY: Marshall Cavendish, 2011.

Steroidology. "Keep Out of Reach of Children—Don Hooton's Crusade to Get Teens Off 'Roids." Steroidology.com, February 26, 2013. Retrieved March 7, 2013 (http://www .steroidology.com/keep-out-of-reach-of-children-don- hootons-crusade-to-get-teens-off-roids).

INDEX

About the Author

Larry Gerber has been reporting on sports and other news for more than forty years. He is a former Associated Press writer and editor and the author of twelve books for young readers. His favorite sports are basketball, skiing, and skating.

Photo Credits

Cover, p. 1 Sean Gallup/Getty Images; pp. 4–5 iStockphoto /Thinkstock; pp. 7, 16, 25, 34, 44, 52, 54, 58, 60, 62 Joe Belanger /Shutterstock.com; p. 8 Alila Medical Images/Shutterstock.com; p. 11 Peter Read Miller/Sports Illustrated/Getty Images; p. 13 © David Hoffman Photo Library/Alamy; p. 15 AFP/Getty Images; p. 17 Tasso Marcelo/AFP/Getty Images; p. 19 Don Emmert/AFP /Getty Images; pp. 21, 28, 41 © AP Images; p. 22 Justin Sullivan /Getty Images; p. 26 © TopFoto/The Image Works; p. 29 Michael Ochs Archives/Moviepix/Getty Images; p. 31 Polk County (Fla.) Sheriff/AP Images; p. 37 © Douglas R. Clifford/Tampa Bay Times/ZUMA Press; p. 38 Biophoto Associates/Science Source; p. 46 New York Daily News/Getty Images; p. 48 Robert Laberge/Getty Images.

Designer: Sam Zavieh; Editor: Kathy Kuhtz Campbell; Photo Researcher: Amy Feinberg